Ping-Pong

Colin Dowland

Illustrated by Jess Mikhail

RIGBY

On Monday, I play ping-pong
with a bat.

But I do not win!

On Tuesday, I play snap
with a crab.

But I do not win!

On Wednesday, I play chess
with a king.

But I do not win!

On Thursday, I play dot-to-dot with a pen.

But I do not win!

On Friday, I play tag
with a dog.

But I do not win!

On Saturday, I play up
with my dad.

But I do not win!

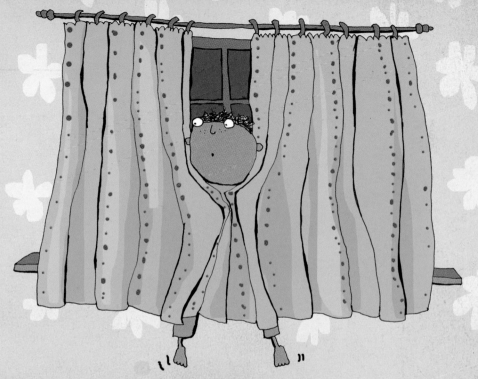

On Sunday, I play IT
with my pet.

And I win!